Cleaning My Room

by Margie Burton, Cathy French, and Tammy Jones

Every Saturday, my mom
comes into my room
to help me clean it up.

One Saturday, she said
that I needed
to sort everything out.

We got to work.

Mom and I put all of my toys into my toy box.

This is a good place for my toys.

My room was looking better.

Next, we went over
to my desk. It was
a real mess. Mom
said that it was time
that I sorted out
my crayons, pencils,
and pens.

She went to get some cups.

Then, I put all of
my crayons into a cup.

I put all of my pens
into a cup.

I put all of my pencils
into a cup.

Now, I have room
to do my work.

Then, we went over to my bookshelf. All of my books and games were on the floor.

It was a real mess!

We put the books and games on the shelves.

Now, I can find my books and games.

Checkers

500 Pc. Jigsaw Puzzle

BOARD GAME

MAGIC KIT

Chess

TRAIN SET

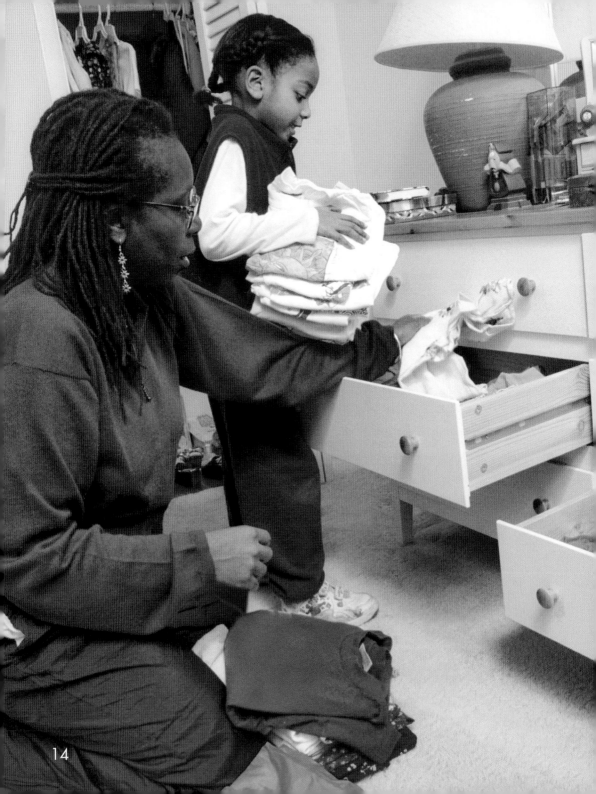

My mom helped me sort out my clothes.

We folded all of my shirts and pants.

Look at my room now.

It looks great.

Thank you, Mom!